Diabetic DESSERTS

Cakes, Pies, Cookies and More!

For the Way You Live

For the Way You Live

Sacrifice no more! Crunchy cookies, decadent cakes, scrumptious cheesecakes, creamy puddings and fruity pies aren't only found in your dreams. Discover the many wonderful recipes this cookbook has to offer and enjoy the simple pleasures in life. With *Diabetic Desserts,* it's easy to make all your dessert fantasies reality.

Facts about the Recipes

The recipes in this publication were selected for people with diabetes in mind. All are based on the principles of sound nutrition as outlined by the Dietary Guidelines developed by the United States Department of Agriculture and the United States Department of Health and Human Services, making them perfect for the entire family. Although the recipes in the publication are not intended as a medically therapeutic program, nor as a substitute for medically approved meal plans for individuals with diabetes, they contain amounts of calories, fat, cholesterol, sodium and sugar that will fit easily into an individualized meal plan designed by your physician, registered dietitian and you.

The ban on sugar has been lifted for people with diabetes, but it is not altogether gone. The new guidelines for sugar intake are based on scientific research that indicates that carbohydrate in the form of sugars does not raise blood sugar levels more rapidly than other types of carbohydrate-containing food. What is more important is the total amount of carbohydrate consumed, not the source. However, keep in mind that sweets and other sugar-containing foods are often high in calories and fat and contain few, if any, other nutrients. If you have any questions or concerns about the use of sugar in your diet, consult your physician and registered dietitian for more information.

Facts about the Exchanges

The nutrition information that appears with each recipe was calculated by an independent nutrition consulting firm, and the Dietary Exchanges are based on the Exchange Lists for Meal Planning developed by the American Diabetes Association/The American Dietetic Association. Every effort has been made to check the accuracy of these numbers. However, because numerous variables account for a wide range of values in certain foods, all analyses that appears in the book should be considered approximate.

- The analysis of each recipe includes all the ingredients that are listed in that recipe, *except* ingredients labeled as "optional" or "for garnish." Nutritional analysis is provided for the primary recipe only, not for the recipe variations.

- If a range is offered for an ingredient, the *first* amount given was used to calculate the nutrition information.

- If an ingredient is presented with an option ("3 tablespoons margarine or butter," for example), the *first* item listed was used to calculate the nutrition information.

Sugar Substitutes

Every recipe in this cookbook using a sugar substitute was developed using aspartame sweetener. Before making any of these recipes, check to see what kind of sugar substitute you are using (aspartame, acesulfame-K or saccharin). Look at the package carefully and use the amount necessary to equal the granulated sugar equivalent called for in each recipe. Follow the chart below for some general measurements.

Amount of Sugar Substitute Packets to Substitute for Granulated Sugar

Granulated Sugar	Aspartame	Acesulfame-K	Saccharin
2 teaspoons	1 packet	1 packet	⅛ teaspoon
1 tablespoon	1½ packets	1¼ packets	⅓ teaspoon
¼ cup	6 packets	3 packets	3 packets
⅓ cup	8 packets	4 packets	4 packets
½ cup	12 packets	6 packets	6 packets

Everyday Delights

Chocolate Fudge Cheesecake Parfaits

1½ **cups nonfat cottage cheese**
  4 **packets sugar substitute** *or* **equivalent of 8 teaspoons sugar**
  2 **teaspoons packed brown sugar**
1½ **teaspoons vanilla**
  2 **tablespoons semisweet mini chocolate chips, divided**
  2 **cups fat-free chocolate ice cream or fat-free frozen yogurt**
  3 **tablespoons graham cracker crumbs**

1. Combine cottage cheese, sugar substitute, brown sugar and vanilla in food processor or blender; process until smooth. Stir in 1 tablespoon mini chips with wooden spoon.

2. Spoon about ¼ cup ice cream into each stemmed glass. Top with heaping tablespoon cheese mixture; sprinkle with 2 teaspoons graham cracker crumbs. Repeat layers. Freeze parfaits 15 to 30 minutes to firm slightly.

3. Garnish each parfait with remaining 1 tablespoon mini chips and remaining cracker crumbs. *Makes 4 servings*

Nutrients per Serving

Calories	199	Saturated Fat	1 g	Cholesterol	0 mg
Calories from Fat	11 %	Protein	17 g	Sodium	419 mg
Total Fat	2 g	Carbohydrate	28 g	Dietary Fiber	1 g

DIETARY EXCHANGES: 1½ Starch, 1½ Lean Meat

Chocolate Fudge Cheesecake Parfaits

Cinnamon Dessert Tacos with Fruit Salsa

1 cup sliced fresh strawberries
1 cup cubed fresh pineapple
1 cup cubed peeled kiwi
½ teaspoon minced jalapeño pepper (optional)
2 packets sugar substitute *or* equivalent of 4 teaspoons sugar (optional)
3 tablespoons sugar
1 tablespoon ground cinnamon
6 (8-inch) flour tortillas
   Nonstick cooking spray

1. Stir together strawberries, pineapple, kiwi, jalapeño pepper and sugar substitute in large bowl; set aside. Combine sugar and cinnamon in small bowl; set aside.

2. Spray tortilla lightly on both sides with nonstick cooking spray. Heat over medium heat in nonstick skillet until slightly puffed and golden brown. Remove from heat; immediately dust both sides with cinnamon-sugar mixture. Shake excess cinnamon-sugar back into small bowl. Repeat cooking and dusting process until all tortillas are warmed.

3. Fold tortillas in half and fill with fruit mixture. Serve immediately.

Makes 6 servings

Nutrients per Serving

Calories	183	Saturated Fat	<1 g	Cholesterol	0 mg
Calories from Fat	14 %	Protein	4 g	Sodium	169 mg
Total Fat	3 g	Carbohydrate	36 g	Dietary Fiber	4 g

DIETARY EXCHANGES: 1½ Starch, 1 Fruit, ½ Fat

Cinnamon Dessert Taco with Fruit Salsa

New Age Candy Apple

1 Granny Smith apple, peeled
¼ teaspoon sugar-free cherry-flavored gelatin
2 tablespoons diet cherry cola
2 tablespoons thawed frozen reduced-fat nondairy whipped
topping

1. Slice apple crosswise into ¼-inch-thick rings; remove seeds. Place stack of apple rings in small microwavable bowl; sprinkle with gelatin. Pour cola over rings.

2. Cover loosely with waxed paper. Microwave at HIGH 2 minutes or until liquid is boiling. Allow to stand, covered, 5 minutes. Arrange rings on dessert plate. Serve warm with whipped topping. *Makes 1 serving*

Note: This recipe can be doubled or tripled easily. To cook 2 apples at a time, increase cooking time to 3½ minutes. To cook 3 apples at a time, increase cooking time to 5 minutes.

Nutrients per Serving

Calories	102	Saturated Fat	1 g	Cholesterol	0 mg
Calories from Fat	17 %	Protein	<1 g	Sodium	1 mg
Total Fat	2 g	Carbohydrate	23 g	Dietary Fiber	4 g

DIETARY EXCHANGES: 1½ Fruit

This recipe works great with any crisp apple. A Jonathan apple will give a tart flavor, a Cortland apple will give a sweet-tart flavor and a Red Delicious apple will give a sweet flavor. Choose your favorite apple and enjoy!

New Age Candy Apple

Rocky Road Pudding

¼ cup sugar
5 tablespoons unsweetened cocoa powder
3 tablespoons cornstarch
⅛ teaspoon salt
2½ cups low-fat (1%) milk
2 egg yolks, beaten
2 teaspoons vanilla
6 packets sugar substitute *or* equivalent of ¼ cup sugar
1 cup miniature marshmallows
¼ cup chopped walnuts, toasted

1. Combine sugar, cocoa, cornstarch and salt in small saucepan; mix well. Stir in milk; cook over medium-high heat, stirring constantly, about 10 minutes or until mixture thickens and begins to boil.

2. Pour about ½ cup pudding mixture over beaten egg yolks in small bowl; beat well. Pour mixture back into saucepan. Cook over medium heat an additional 10 minutes. Remove from heat; stir in vanilla.

3. Place plastic wrap on surface of pudding. Refrigerate about 20 minutes or until slightly cooled. Remove plastic wrap; stir in sugar substitute. Spoon pudding into 6 dessert dishes; top with marshmallows and nuts. Serve warm or cold.

Makes 6 servings

Nutrients per Serving

Calories	190	Saturated Fat	1 g	Cholesterol	75 mg
Calories from Fat	27 %	Protein	7 g	Sodium	121 mg
Total Fat	6 g	Carbohydrate	28 g	Dietary Fiber	<1 g

DIETARY EXCHANGES: 1 Starch, ½ Milk, 1 Fat

Cranberry-Orange Bread Pudding

2 cups cubed cinnamon bread
¼ cup dried cranberries
2 cups low-fat (1%) milk
1 package (4 serving size) sugar-free vanilla pudding and pie filling mix*
½ cup cholesterol-free egg substitute
1 teaspoon vanilla
1 teaspoon grated orange peel
½ teaspoon ground cinnamon
Low-fat no-sugar-added vanilla ice cream (optional)

Do not use instant pudding and pie filling.

1. Preheat oven to 325°F. Spray 9 custard cups with nonstick cooking spray.

2. Place bread cubes in custard cups. Bake 10 minutes; add cranberries.

3. Combine remaining ingredients except ice cream in medium bowl. Carefully pour over mixture in custard cups. Let stand 5 to 10 minutes.

4. Place cups on baking sheet; bake 25 to 30 minutes or until center is almost set. Let stand 10 minutes. Serve with ice cream, if desired.

Makes 9 servings

Nutrients per Serving

Calories	67	Saturated Fat	<1 g	Cholesterol	2 mg
Calories from Fat	13 %	Protein	4 g	Sodium	190 mg
Total Fat	1 g	Carbohydrate	11 g	Dietary Fiber	<1 g

DIETARY EXCHANGES: 1 Starch

Orange Smoothies

1 cup fat-free vanilla ice cream or fat-free vanilla frozen yogurt
¾ cup low-fat (1%) milk
¼ cup frozen orange juice concentrate

1. Combine ice cream, milk and orange juice concentrate in food processor or blender; process until smooth.

2. Pour mixture into 2 glasses; garnish as desired. Serve immediately.

Makes 2 servings

Nutrients per Serving

Calories	185	Saturated Fat	<1 g	Cholesterol	4 mg
Calories from Fat	5 %	Protein	8 g	Sodium	117 mg
Total Fat	1 g	Carbohydrate	38 g	Dietary Fiber	<1 g

DIETARY EXCHANGES: 1½ Starch, 1 Fruit

Raspberry Smoothies

1 cup plain nonfat yogurt with aspartame sweetener
1 cup crushed ice
1½ cups fresh or frozen raspberries
1 tablespoon honey
2 packets sugar substitute *or* equivalent of 4 teaspoons sugar

1. Place all ingredients in food processor or blender; process until smooth. Scrape down sides as needed. Serve immediately.

Makes 2 servings

Nutrients per Serving

Calories	143	Saturated Fat	<1 g	Cholesterol	2 mg
Calories from Fat	4 %	Protein	8 g	Sodium	88 mg
Total Fat	<1 g	Carbohydrate	28 g	Dietary Fiber	6 g

DIETARY EXCHANGES: ½ Milk, 1½ Fruit

Orange Smoothies

Sugar Cookie Fruit Tart

1 package (about 18 ounces) refrigerated sugar cookie dough
1 package (8 ounces) fat-free cream cheese, softened
¼ cup orange marmalade
1 teaspoon vanilla
2 packets sugar substitute *or* equivalent of 4 teaspoons sugar, divided
1 can (11 ounces) mandarin oranges, drained
16 strawberries, halved
1 kiwi, peeled, sliced and halved

1. Preheat oven 350°F. Coat 12-inch pizza pan with nonstick cooking spray; set aside.

2. Slice dough into 16 slices. Arrange cookie slices ½ inch apart on prepared pan. Press cookie dough to cover bottom and sides of pizza pan evenly. Spray fingertips with nonstick cooking spray to prevent sticking if needed.

3. Bake 20 to 22 minutes or until golden brown. Cool completely in pan on wire rack.

4. Beat cream cheese, marmalade, vanilla and 1 packet sugar substitute in medium bowl with electric mixer at high speed until well blended; refrigerate.

5. To assemble, spread cream cheese mixture on top of cooled cookie crust. Mix fruit with remaining packet sugar substitute. Arrange fruit on top of cream cheese mixture. Serve immediately or cover with plastic wrap and refrigerate.

Makes 12 servings

Nutrients per Serving

Calories	265	Saturated Fat	3 g	Cholesterol	15 mg
Calories from Fat	34 %	Protein	5 g	Sodium	304 mg
Total Fat	10 g	Carbohydrate	39 g	Dietary Fiber	2 g

DIETARY EXCHANGES: 1½ Starch, 1 Fruit, 2 Fat

Sugar Cookie Fruit Tart

Iced Cappuccino

  1 cup fat-free vanilla frozen yogurt or fat-free vanilla ice cream
  1 cup cold strong-brewed coffee
  1 teaspoon unsweetened cocoa powder
  1 teaspoon vanilla
  1 packet sugar substitute *or* equivalent of 2 teaspoons sugar

1. Place all ingredients in food processor or blender; process until smooth. Place container in freezer; freeze 1½ to 2 hours or until top and sides of mixture are partially frozen.

2. Scrape sides of container; process until smooth and frothy. Garnish as desired. Serve immediately.   *Makes 2 servings*

Iced Mocha Cappuccino: Increase amount of unsweetened cocoa powder to 1 tablespoon. Proceed as above.

Nutrients per Serving

Calories	105	Saturated Fat	<1 g	Cholesterol	<1 mg
Calories from Fat	0 %	Protein	5 g	Sodium	72 mg
Total Fat	<1 g	Carbohydrate	21 g	Dietary Fiber	0 g

DIETARY EXCHANGES: 1½ Starch

*To add an extra flavor boost to this refreshing drink,
add orange peel, lemon peel or a dash of ground
cinnamon to your coffee grounds before brewing.*

Iced Cappuccino

Cookies & Bars

Cream Cheese Brownie Royale

> 1 package (about 15 ounces) low-fat brownie mix
> ⅔ cup cold coffee or water
> 1 package (8 ounces) reduced-fat cream cheese, softened
> ¼ cup fat-free (skim) milk
> 5 packets sugar substitute *or* equivalent of 10 teaspoons sugar
> ½ teaspoon vanilla

1. Preheat oven to 350°F. Coat 13×9-inch nonstick baking pan with nonstick cooking spray; set aside.

2. Combine brownie mix and coffee in large bowl; stir until blended. Pour brownie mixture into prepared pan.

3. Beat cream cheese, milk, sugar substitute and vanilla in medium bowl with electric mixer at medium speed until smooth. Spoon cream cheese mixture in dollops over brownie mixture. Swirl cream cheese mixture into brownie mixture with tip of knife.

4. Bake 30 to 35 minutes or until toothpick inserted in center comes out clean. Cool completely in pan on wire rack.

5. Cover with foil and refrigerate 8 hours or until ready to serve. Garnish as desired.   *Makes 16 servings*

Nutrients per Serving

Calories	143	Saturated Fat	2 g	Cholesterol	7 mg
Calories from Fat	26%	Protein	3 g	Sodium	161 mg
Total Fat	4 g	Carbohydrate	23 g	Dietary Fiber	1 g

DIETARY EXCHANGES: 1½ Starch, ½ Fat

Cream Cheese Brownie Royale

Apple-Cranberry Crescent Cookies

1¼ cups chopped apples
½ cup dried cranberries
½ cup reduced-fat sour cream
¼ cup cholesterol-free egg substitute
¼ cup margarine or butter, melted
3 tablespoons sugar, divided
1 package quick-rise yeast
1 teaspoon vanilla
2 cups all-purpose flour
1 teaspoon ground cinnamon
1 tablespoon reduced-fat (2%) milk

1. Preheat oven to 350°F. Lightly coat cookie sheet with nonstick cooking spray; set aside.

2. Place apples and cranberries in food processor or blender; pulse to finely chop. Set aside.

3. Combine sour cream, egg substitute, margarine and 2 tablespoons sugar in medium bowl. Add yeast and vanilla. Add flour; stir to form ball. Turn dough out onto lightly floured work surface. Knead 1 minute. Cover with plastic wrap; allow to stand 10 minutes.

4. Divide dough into thirds. Roll one portion to 12-inch circle. Spread with ⅓ apple mixture (about ¼ cup). Cut dough to make 8 wedges. Roll up each wedge beginning at outside edge. Place on prepared cookie sheet; turn ends of cookies to form crescents. Repeat with remaining dough and apple mixture.

5. Combine remaining 1 tablespoon sugar and cinnamon in small bowl. Lightly brush cookies with milk; sprinkle with sugar-cinnamon mixture. Bake cookies 18 to 20 minutes or until lightly browned.   *Makes 24 servings*

Nutrients per Serving

Calories	82	Saturated Fat	1 g	Cholesterol	2 mg
Calories from Fat	27 %	Protein	2 g	Sodium	31 mg
Total Fat	2 g	Carbohydrate	13 g	Dietary Fiber	1 g

DIETARY EXCHANGES: 1 Starch

Apple-Cranberry Crescent Cookies

Carrot & Spice Bars

1 cup low-fat (1%) milk
¼ cup margarine or butter
1 cup bran flakes cereal
2 eggs
1 jar (2½ ounces) puréed baby food carrots
¾ cup grated carrot
⅓ cup golden raisins, coarsely chopped
1 teaspoon grated orange peel
1 teaspoon vanilla
2 cups all-purpose flour
¾ cup sugar
1 teaspoon baking soda
1 teaspoon ground cinnamon
¼ cup orange juice
¼ cup toasted pecans, chopped

1. Preheat oven to 350°F. Lightly coat 13×9-inch baking pan with nonstick cooking spray; set aside.

2. Combine milk and margarine in large microwavable bowl. Microwave at HIGH 1 minute or until margarine is melted; add cereal. Let stand 5 minutes. Add eggs; whisk to blend. Add puréed carrots, grated carrot, raisins, orange peel and vanilla.

3. Combine flour, sugar, baking soda and cinnamon in medium bowl. Add to carrot mixture, stirring just until thoroughly blended. Spread into prepared pan.

4. Bake 25 minutes or until toothpick inserted in center comes out clean. Insert tines of fork into cake at 1-inch intervals. Spoon orange juice over cake. Sprinkle with pecans; press into cake.   *Makes 40 servings*

Nutrients per Serving

Calories	114	Saturated Fat	1 g	Cholesterol	18 mg
Calories from Fat	26 %	Protein	2 g	Sodium	100 mg
Total Fat	3 g	Carbohydrate	19 g	Dietary Fiber	1 g

DIETARY EXCHANGES: 1 Starch, 1½ Fruit, ½ Fat

Butterscotch Bars

¾ **cup all-purpose flour**
½ **cup packed brown sugar**
½ **cup fat-free butterscotch ice cream topping**
3 **tablespoons margarine or butter, melted**
¼ **cup cholesterol-free egg substitute**
1 **teaspoon vanilla**
¼ **teaspoon salt**
½ **cup toasted chopped pecans (optional)**

1. Preheat oven to 350°F. Lightly coat 8-inch square baking pan with nonstick cooking spray; set aside.

2. Combine all ingredients in medium bowl; stir until blended. Spread into prepared pan.

3. Bake 15 to 18 minutes or until firm to touch. Cool completely in pan. Cut into 16 bars.   *Makes 16 servings*

Nutrients per Serving

Calories	95	Saturated Fat	<1 g	Cholesterol	<1 mg
Calories from Fat	20 %	Protein	1 g	Sodium	107 mg
Total Fat	2 g	Carbohydrate	18 g	Dietary Fiber	<1 g

DIETARY EXCHANGES: 1 Starch, ½ Fat

These sweet bars are the perfect packable treat. Wrap individually in plastic wrap and they are ready to grab for the lunch box or a spur of the moment picnic in the park.

Apricot Biscotti

   3 cups all-purpose flour
1½ teaspoons baking soda
   ½ teaspoon salt
   3 eggs
   ⅔ cup sugar
   1 teaspoon vanilla
   ½ cup chopped dried apricots*
   ⅓ cup sliced almonds, chopped
   1 tablespoon reduced-fat (2%) milk

Other chopped dried fruits, such as dried cherries, cranberries or blueberries, may be substituted.

1. Preheat oven to 350°F. Lightly coat cookie sheet with nonstick cooking spray; set aside.

2. Combine flour, baking soda and salt in medium bowl; set aside.

3. Beat eggs, sugar and vanilla in large bowl with electric mixer at medium speed until combined. Add flour mixture; beat well.

4. Stir in apricots and almonds. Turn dough out onto lightly floured work surface. Knead 4 to 6 times. Roll dough into 20-inch log; place on prepared cookie sheet. Brush dough with milk.

5. Bake 30 minutes or until firm to touch. Remove from oven; cool 10 minutes. Diagonally slice into 30 biscotti. Place slices on cookie sheet. Bake 10 minutes; turn and bake an additional 10 minutes. Cool on wire racks. Store in airtight container.   *Makes 30 servings*

Nutrients per Serving

Calories	86	Saturated Fat	<1 g	Cholesterol	21 mg
Calories from Fat	13 %	Protein	2 g	Sodium	108 mg
Total Fat	1 g	Carbohydrate	16 g	Dietary Fiber	1 g

DIETARY EXCHANGES: 1 Starch

Apricot Biscotti

Oatmeal-Date Cookies

½ cup packed light brown sugar
¼ cup margarine, softened
1 whole egg
1 egg white
1 tablespoon thawed frozen apple juice concentrate
1 teaspoon vanilla
1½ cups all-purpose flour
2 teaspoons baking soda
¼ teaspoon salt
1½ cups uncooked quick oats
½ cup chopped dates or raisins

1. Preheat oven to 350°F. Lightly coat cookie sheet with nonstick cooking spray; set aside.

2. Combine sugar and margarine in large bowl; mix well. Add egg, egg white, apple juice concentrate and vanilla; mix well.

3. Add flour, baking soda and salt; mix well. Stir in oats and dates. Drop dough by teaspoons onto prepared cookie sheet.

4. Bake 8 to 10 minutes or until edges are very lightly browned; center should still be soft.

5. Cool 1 minute on cookie sheet; remove to wire rack and cool completely.

Makes 36 servings

Nutrients per Serving

Calories	65	Saturated Fat	<1 g	Cholesterol	6 mg
Calories from Fat	27 %	Protein	1 g	Sodium	106 mg
Total Fat	2 g	Carbohydrate	11 g	Dietary Fiber	1 g

DIETARY EXCHANGES: 1 Starch

Oatmeal-Date Cookies

Fig Bars

DOUGH
- ½ **cup dried figs**
- 6 **tablespoons hot water**
- 1 **tablespoon sugar**
- ⅔ **cup all-purpose flour**
- ½ **cup uncooked quick oats**
- ¾ **teaspoon baking powder**
- ¼ **teaspoon salt**
- 2 **tablespoons oil**
- 3 **tablespoons fat-free (skim) milk**

ICING
- 1 **ounce reduced-fat cream cheese**
- ⅓ **cup powdered sugar**
- ½ **teaspoon vanilla**

1. Preheat oven to 400°F. Lightly coat cookie sheet with nonstick cooking spray; set aside.

2. To prepare dough, combine figs, water and sugar in food processor or blender; process until figs are finely chopped. Set aside. Combine flour, oats, baking powder and salt in medium bowl. Add oil and just enough milk, 1 tablespoon at a time, until mixture forms a ball.

3. On lightly floured surface, roll dough into 12×9-inch rectangle. Place dough on prepared cookie sheet. Spread fig mixture in 2½-inch-wide strip lengthwise down center of rectangle. Make cuts almost to filling at ½-inch intervals on both 12-inch sides. Fold strips over filling, overlapping and crossing in center. Bake 15 to 18 minutes or until lightly browned.

4. To prepare icing, combine all ingredients in small bowl; mix well. Drizzle over braid. Cut into 12 pieces. *Makes 12 servings*

Nutrients per Serving

Calories	104	Saturated Fat	1 g	Cholesterol	1 mg
Calories from Fat	26 %	Protein	2 g	Sodium	93 mg
Total Fat	3 g	Carbohydrate	18 g	Dietary Fiber	1 g

DIETARY EXCHANGES: 1 Starch, ½ Fat

Peanut Butter Cereal Bars

3 cups miniature marshmallows
3 tablespoons margarine
½ cup reduced-fat peanut butter
3½ cups crisp rice cereal
1 cup uncooked quick oats
⅓ cup mini semisweet chocolate chips

1. Lightly coat 13×9-inch baking pan with nonstick cooking spray; set aside.

2. Combine marshmallows and margarine in large microwavable bowl. Microwave at HIGH 15 seconds; stir. Continue to microwave 1 minute; stir until marshmallows are melted and mixture is smooth. Add peanut butter; stir. Add cereal and oats; stir until well coated. Spread into prepared pan. Immediately sprinkle chocolate chips on top; lightly press.

3. Cool completely in pan. Cut into 40 bars.   *Makes 40 servings*

Nutrients per Serving

Calories	65	Saturated Fat	1 g	Cholesterol	0 mg
Calories from Fat	41 %	Protein	1 g	Sodium	58 mg
Total Fat	3 g	Carbohydrate	10 g	Dietary Fiber	1 g

DIETARY EXCHANGES: ½ Starch, ½ Fat

To make spreading the cereal mixture easier and cleanup a snap, lightly spray your spoon with nonstick cooking spray before stirring these bars.

Lemon-Cranberry Bars

½ **cup frozen lemonade concentrate, thawed**
½ **cup spoonable sugar substitute**
¼ **cup margarine**
1 **egg**
1½ **cups all-purpose flour**
2 **teaspoons grated lemon peel**
½ **teaspoon baking soda**
½ **teaspoon salt**
½ **cup dried cranberries**

1. Preheat oven to 375°F. Lightly coat 8-inch square baking pan with nonstick cooking spray; set aside.

2. Combine lemonade concentrate, sugar substitute, margarine and egg in medium bowl; mix well. Add flour, lemon peel, baking soda and salt; stir well. Stir in cranberries; pour into prepared pan.

3. Bake 20 minutes or until light brown. Cool completely in pan on wire rack. Cut into 16 squares.   *Makes 16 servings*

Nutrients per Serving

Calories	104	Saturated Fat	1 g	Cholesterol	13 mg
Calories from Fat	28 %	Protein	3 g	Sodium	150 mg
Total Fat	3 g	Carbohydrate	15 g	Dietary Fiber	<1 g

DIETARY EXCHANGES: 1 Starch, ½ Fat

Lemon-Cranberry Bars

Pumpkin & Chocolate Chip Cookies

2 cups all-purpose flour
1 teaspoon baking soda
1 teaspoon ground cinnamon
½ teaspoon salt
¼ teaspoon ground nutmeg
¼ teaspoon ground cloves
½ cup solid-pack pumpkin
½ cup packed brown sugar
½ cup granulated sugar
¼ cup caramel-flavored low-fat yogurt
1 egg
½ cup mini semisweet chocolate chips

1. Preheat oven to 350°F. Lightly coat cookie sheet with nonstick cooking spray; set aside.

2. Combine flour, baking soda, cinnamon, salt, nutmeg and cloves in medium bowl; set aside.

3. Combine pumpkin, sugars, yogurt and egg in large bowl. Blend in flour mixture. Add chocolate chips.

4. Drop dough by teaspoons onto prepared cookie sheet. Bake 10 minutes or until firm to touch. Remove to wire rack and cool completely.

Makes 36 servings

Nutrients per Serving

Calories	63	Saturated Fat	<1 g	Cholesterol	6 mg
Calories from Fat	14 %	Protein	1 g	Sodium	72 mg
Total Fat	1 g	Carbohydrate	13 g	Dietary Fiber	<1 g

DIETARY EXCHANGES: 1 Starch

Confetti Cookies

2⅓ cups all purpose flour
1½ teaspoons baking soda
¼ teaspoon salt
¼ cup margarine or butter, softened
3 ounces reduced-fat cream cheese
¾ cup sugar
¼ cup cholesterol-free egg substitute
½ teaspoon almond extract
1 cup dried fruit bits
Sliced almonds (optional)

1. Combine flour, baking soda and salt in medium bowl; set aside.

2. Beat margarine and cream cheese in large bowl with electric mixer at medium speed until blended. Add sugar, egg substitute and almond extract; beat until well blended. Stir in dry ingredients; add fruit bits.

3. Shape dough into 2 logs, each about 9 inches long. Wrap each log in waxed paper or plastic wrap. Refrigerate 1 hour or overnight.

4. Preheat oven to 350°F. Lightly coat cookie sheet with nonstick cooking spray. Cut logs into ½-inch-thick slices. Place on prepared cookie sheet. Arrange three almond slices on top of each cookie in decorative pattern. Bake 10 minutes or until firm to touch. Remove to wire rack and cool completely.

Makes 36 servings

Nutrients per Serving

Calories	74	Saturated Fat	1 g	Cholesterol	1 mg
Calories from Fat	24 %	Protein	1 g	Sodium	98 mg
Total Fat	2 g	Carbohydrate	13 g	Dietary Fiber	1 g

DIETARY EXCHANGES: 1 Starch

Thumbprint Cookies

1½ cups all-purpose flour
1 teaspoon baking soda
¼ teaspoon salt
⅔ cup sugar
¼ cup margarine, softened
1 egg white
1 teaspoon vanilla
½ cup no-sugar-added raspberry or apricot fruit spread

1. Combine flour, baking soda and salt in medium bowl; set aside. Beat sugar, margarine, egg white and vanilla in large bowl with electric mixer at high speed until blended. Add flour mixture; mix well. Press mixture together to form a ball. Refrigerate ½ hour or overnight.

2. Preheat oven to 375°F. Lightly coat cookie sheet with nonstick cooking spray; set aside.

3. Shape dough into 1-inch balls with lightly floured hands; place on cookie sheet. Press down with thumb in center of each ball to form indention.

4. Bake 10 to 12 minutes or until golden brown. Remove to wire rack and cool completely. Fill each indention with about 1 teaspoon fruit spread.

Makes 20 servings

Nutrients per Serving

Calories	90	Saturated Fat	<1 g	Cholesterol	0 mg
Calories from Fat	24 %	Protein	1 g	Sodium	130 mg
Total Fat	2 g	Carbohydrate	16 g	Dietary Fiber	<1 g

DIETARY EXCHANGES: 1 Starch, ½ Fat

Thumbprint Cookies

Hikers' Bar Cookies

¾ cup all-purpose flour
½ cup packed brown sugar
½ cup uncooked quick oats
¼ cup toasted wheat germ
¼ cup unsweetened applesauce
¼ cup margarine or butter, softened
⅛ teaspoon salt
½ cup cholesterol-free egg substitute
¼ cup raisins
¼ cup dried cranberries
¼ cup sunflower kernels
1 tablespoon orange peel
1 teaspoon ground cinnamon

1. Preheat oven to 350°F. Lightly coat 13×9-inch baking pan with nonstick cooking spray; set aside.

2. Beat flour, sugar, oats, wheat germ, applesauce, margarine and salt in large bowl with electric mixer at medium speed until well blended. Add egg substitute, raisins, cranberries, sunflower kernels, orange peel and cinnamon. Spread into pan.

3. Bake 15 minutes or until firm to touch. Cool completely in pan on wire rack. Cut into 24 squares. *Makes 24 servings*

Nutrients per Serving

Calories	80	Saturated Fat	<1 g	Cholesterol	0 mg
Calories from Fat	33 %	Protein	2 g	Sodium	46 mg
Total Fat	3 g	Carbohydrate	12 g	Dietary Fiber	1 g

DIETARY EXCHANGES: 1 Starch, ½ Fat

Hikers' Bar Cookies

Cakes & Cheesecakes

Cherry Bowl Cheesecakes

    1 package (8 ounces) fat-free cream cheese, softened
    1 package (8 ounces) reduced-fat cream cheese, softened
    2 tablespoons fat-free (skim) milk
    4 packets sugar substitute *or* equivalent of 8 teaspoons sugar
    ¼ teaspoon almond extract
  40 reduced-fat vanilla wafers
    1 can (16 ounces) light cherry pie filling

1. Beat cream cheese, milk, sugar substitute and almond extract in medium bowl with electric mixer at high speed until well blended.

2. Place one vanilla wafer on bottom of 4-ounce ramekin.* Arrange four additional vanilla wafers around side of ramekin. Repeat with remaining wafers. Fill each ramekin with ¼ cup cream cheese mixture; top each with ¼ cup cherry pie filling. Cover with plastic wrap; refrigerate 8 hours or overnight.   *Makes 8 servings*

*Note: If ramekins are not available, you may substitute with custard dishes or line 8 muffin cups with paper liners and fill according to above directions.

Nutrients per Serving

Calories	214	Saturated Fat	4 g	Cholesterol	16 mg
Calories from Fat	29 %	Protein	9 g	Sodium	387 mg
Total Fat	7 g	Carbohydrate	29 g	Dietary Fiber	1 g

DIETARY EXCHANGES: 1 Starch, 1 Fruit, 1½ Fat

Cherry Bowl Cheesecake

Chocolate Bundt Cake with White Chocolate Glaze

CAKE

    1 package (18.25 ounces) chocolate cake mix
    3 whole eggs *or* ¾ cup cholesterol-free egg substitute
    3 jars (2½ ounces each) puréed baby food prunes
    ¾ cup warm water
    2 to 3 teaspoons instant coffee granules
    2 tablespoons canola oil

GLAZE

    ½ cup white chocolate chips
    1 tablespoon milk

1. Preheat oven to 350°F. Lightly grease and flour Bundt pan; set aside.

2. Beat all ingredients for Bundt cake in large bowl with electric mixer at high speed 2 minutes. Pour into prepared pan. Bake 40 minutes or until toothpick inserted in center comes out clean; cool 10 minutes. Invert cake onto serving plate; cool completely.

3. To prepare glaze, combine white chocolate chips and milk in small microwavable bowl. Microwave at MEDIUM (50% power) 50 seconds; stir. Microwave at MEDIUM at additional 30-second intervals until chips are completely melted; stir well after each 30 second interval.

4. Pour warm glaze over cooled cake. Let stand about 30 minutes. Garnish as desired; serve. *Makes 16 servings*

Nutrients per Serving

Calories	209	Saturated Fat	3 g	Cholesterol	41 mg
Calories from Fat	33 %	Protein	3 g	Sodium	259 mg
Total Fat	8 g	Carbohydrate	32 g	Dietary Fiber	1 g

DIETARY EXCHANGES: 2 Starch, 1½ Fat

Chocolate Bundt Cake with
White Chocolate Glaze

New-Fashioned Gingerbread Cake

2 cups cake flour
1 teaspoon baking powder
1 teaspoon ground ginger
½ teaspoon baking soda
½ teaspoon ground cinnamon
½ teaspoon ground nutmeg
¼ teaspoon ground cloves
¾ cup water
⅓ cup packed brown sugar
¼ cup molasses
3 tablespoons canola oil
2 tablespoons finely minced crystallized ginger (optional)
2 tablespoons powdered sugar

1. Preheat oven to 350°F. Coat 8-inch square baking pan with nonstick cooking spray; set aside.

2. Combine flour, baking powder, ginger, baking soda, cinnamon, nutmeg and cloves in large bowl; mix well.

3. Beat water, brown sugar, molasses and oil in small bowl with electric mixer at low speed until well blended. Pour into flour mixture; beat until just blended. Stir in crystallized ginger.

4. Pour into prepared pan. Bake 30 to 35 minutes or until toothpick inserted in center comes out clean. Let cool 10 minutes. Sprinkle with powdered sugar just before serving. *Makes 9 servings*

Nutrients per Serving

Calories	188	Saturated Fat	<1 g	Cholesterol	0 mg
Calories from Fat	23 %	Protein	2 g	Sodium	133 mg
Total Fat	5 g	Carbohydrate	34 g	Dietary Fiber	1 g

DIETARY EXCHANGES: 2 Starch, 1 Fat

Chocolate Pudding Cake

CAKE
   1 cup all-purpose flour
   ⅓ cup sugar
  10 packets sugar substitute *or* equivalent of 20 teaspoons sugar
   3 tablespoons unsweetened cocoa
   2 teaspoons baking powder
   ½ teaspoon salt
   2 tablespoons canola oil
   2 teaspoons vanilla

SAUCE
   ¼ cup sugar
  10 packets sugar substitute *or* equivalent of 20 teaspoons sugar
   3 tablespoons unsweetened cocoa
  1¾ cups boiling water

1. Preheat oven to 350°F. Combine all cake ingredients in large bowl; mix well. Pour into ungreased 9-inch square baking pan.

2. To prepare sauce, sprinkle ¼ cup sugar, 10 packets sugar substitute and 3 tablespoons cocoa over batter in pan. Pour boiling water over top. *(Do not stir.)*

3. Bake 40 minutes or until cake portion has risen to top of pan and sauce is bubbling underneath. Serve immediately. *Makes 9 servings*

Nutrients per Serving

Calories	145	Saturated Fat	<1 g	Cholesterol	<1 mg
Calories from Fat	20 %	Protein	4 g	Sodium	245 mg
Total Fat	3 g	Carbohydrate	25 g	Dietary Fiber	<1 g

DIETARY EXCHANGES: 1½ Starch, ½ Fat

Luscious Lime Angel Food Cake Rolls

1 package (16 ounces) angel food cake mix
2 cartons (8 ounces each) lime-flavored nonfat yogurt with
**   aspartame sweetener**
2 drops green food coloring (optional)
**   Lime slices (optional)**

1. Preheat oven to 350°F. Line two 17×11¼×1-inch jelly roll pans with parchment or waxed paper; set aside.

2. Prepare angel food cake batter according to package directions. Divide batter evenly between prepared pans. Draw knife through batter to remove large air bubbles. Bake 12 minutes or until cakes are lightly browned and toothpick inserted in centers comes out clean.

3. Invert each cake onto separate clean towel. Starting at short end, roll warm cake, jelly-roll fashion with towel inside. Cool cakes completely.

4. Place 1 to 2 drops green food coloring in each carton of yogurt; stir well. Unroll cake; remove towel. Spread each cake with 1 carton yogurt, leaving 1-inch border. Roll up cake; place seam side down. Slice each cake roll into 8 pieces. Garnish with lime slices. Refrigerate if not serving immediately.

Makes 16 servings

Nutrients per Serving

Calories	136	Saturated Fat	<1 g	Cholesterol	0 mg
Calories from Fat	1 %	Protein	4 g	Sodium	252 mg
Total Fat	<1 g	Carbohydrate	30 g	Dietary Fiber	<1 g

DIETARY EXCHANGES: 2 Starch

Luscious Lime Angel Food Cake Roll

Ginger-Crusted Pumpkin Cheesecake

12 whole low-fat honey graham crackers, broken into pieces
3 tablespoons reduced-fat margarine, melted
½ teaspoon ground ginger
1 can (15 ounces) solid-pack pumpkin
2 packages (8 ounces each) fat-free cream cheese, softened
1 package (8 ounces) reduced-fat cream cheese, softened
1 cup sugar
1 cup cholesterol-free egg substitute
½ cup nonfat evaporated milk
1 tablespoon vanilla
1 teaspoon ground cinnamon
½ teaspoon ground nutmeg
¼ teaspoon salt
2 cups thawed frozen reduced-fat whipped topping
    Additional ground nutmeg (optional)

1. Preheat oven 350°F. Coat 9-inch springform baking pan with nonstick cooking spray; set aside.

2. Place graham crackers, margarine and ginger in food processor or blender; pulse until coarse in texture. Gently press crumb mixture onto bottom and ¾ inch up side of pan. Bake 10 minutes or until lightly browned; cool slightly on wire rack.

3. Beat remaining ingredients except whipped topping and additional nutmeg in large bowl with electric mixer at medium-high speed until smooth; pour into pie crust. Bake 1 hour and 15 minutes or until top begins to crack and center moves very little when pan is shaken back and forth. Cool on wire rack to room temperature; refrigerate until ready to serve.

4. Just before serving, spoon 1 tablespoon whipped topping on each serving; sprinkle lightly with additional nutmeg.

Makes 16 servings

Nutrients per Serving

Calories	187	Saturated Fat	4 g	Cholesterol	9 mg
Calories from Fat	32 %	Protein	8 g	Sodium	338 mg
Total Fat	6 g	Carbohydrate	23 g	Dietary Fiber	1 g

DIETARY EXCHANGES: 1½ Starch, 1 Lean Meat, ½ Fat

Ginger-Crusted Pumpkin Cheesecake

Skinny Carrot Cupcakes with Cream Cheese Frosting

CUPCAKES
- 2½ cups all-purpose flour
- 1¼ cups packed brown sugar
- 2 teaspoons baking powder
- 2 teaspoons ground cinnamon
- 1 teaspoon baking soda
- 1 teaspoon salt
- 1 teaspoon ground ginger
- ½ teaspoon ground cloves
- ½ cup unsweetened applesauce
- ½ cup crushed pineapple in juice
- 1 jar (4 ounces) puréed baby food carrots
- 2 jars (2.5 ounces each) puréed baby food prunes
- ¼ cup canola oil
- ¼ cup buttermilk
- 1 egg
- 2 teaspoons vanilla
- 2 teaspoons grated orange peel

CREAM CHEESE FROSTING
- ¼ cup nonfat cottage cheese
- 6 ounces Neufchâtel cheese
- 2 tablespoons powdered sugar
- 4 packets sugar substitute *or* equivalent of 8 teaspoons sugar
- 1 teaspoon vanilla

1. Preheat oven to 375°F. Line 18 (2½-inch) muffin cups with paper liners; set aside.

2. To prepare cupcakes, stir together flour, brown sugar, baking powder, cinnamon, baking soda, salt, ginger and cloves in large bowl. Add remaining cupcake ingredients; stir just until combined. Spoon evenly into prepared muffin cups.

3. Bake 20 to 25 minutes or until toothpick inserted into center comes out clean. Cool completely before frosting.

4. To prepare frosting, combine cottage cheese, Neufchâtel cheese, powdered sugar, sugar substitute and 1 teaspoon vanilla in food processor or blender; blend until smooth. Frost each cupcake with about 2 teaspoons frosting.

Makes 18 servings

Nutrients per Serving

Calories	202	Saturated Fat	2 g	Cholesterol	19 mg
Calories from Fat	25 %	Protein	4 g	Sodium	320 mg
Total Fat	6 g	Carbohydrate	34 g	Dietary Fiber	1 g

DIETARY EXCHANGES: 2 Starch, 1 Fat

If you don't have buttermilk on hand, you can sour fresh milk to use as a substitute. For ¼ cup of buttermilk, place ½ plus ¼ teaspoon lemon juice or distilled vinegar in a measuring cup and add enough milk to measure ¼ cup. Stir and let mixture stand at room temperature for 5 minutes.

Lemon Poppy Seed Bundt Cake

1 cup granulated sugar
½ cup (1 stick) margarine, softened
1 egg, at room temperature
2 egg whites, at room temperature
¾ cup low-fat (1%) milk
2 teaspoons vanilla
2 cups all-purpose flour
2 tablespoons poppy seeds
1 tablespoon grated lemon peel
2 teaspoons baking powder
¼ teaspoon salt
1½ tablespoons powdered sugar

1. Preheat oven to 350°F. Grease and flour Bundt pan; set aside.

2. Beat granulated sugar, margarine, egg and egg whites in large bowl with electric mixer at medium speed until well blended. Add milk and vanilla; mix well. Add flour, poppy seeds, lemon peel, baking powder and salt; beat about 2 minutes or until smooth.

3. Pour into prepared pan. Bake 30 minutes or until toothpick inserted into center comes out clean. Gently loosen cake from pan with knife and turn out onto wire rack; cool completely. Sprinkle with powdered sugar. Garnish as desired.
Makes 16 servings

Nutrients per Serving

Calories	178	Saturated Fat	1 g	Cholesterol	14 mg
Calories from Fat	34 %	Protein	3 g	Sodium	181 mg
Total Fat	7 g	Carbohydrate	26 g	Dietary Fiber	1 g

DIETARY EXCHANGES: 1½ Starch, 1½ Fat

Lemon Poppy Seed Bundt Cake

Boston Babies

    1 package (18.25 ounces) yellow cake mix
    3 eggs *or* ¾ cup cholesterol-free egg substitute
    ⅓ cup unsweetened applesauce
    1 package (4 serving size) sugar-free vanilla pudding and pie filling
        mix
    2 cups low-fat (1%) milk or fat-free (skim) milk
    ⅓ cup sugar
    ⅓ cup unsweetened cocoa powder
    1 tablespoon cornstarch
    1½ cups water
    1½ teaspoons vanilla

1. Line 24 (2½-inch) muffin cups with paper liners; set aside.

2. Prepare cake mix according to lower fat package directions, using 3 eggs and applesauce. Pour batter into prepared muffin cups. Bake according to package directions; cool completely. Freeze 12 cupcakes for future use.

3. Prepare pudding according to package directions, using 2 cups milk; cover and refrigerate.

4. Combine sugar, cocoa, cornstarch and water in large microwavable bowl; whisk until smooth. Microwave at HIGH 4 to 6 minutes, stirring every 2 minutes, until slightly thickened. Stir in vanilla.

5. To serve, drizzle 2 tablespoons chocolate glaze over each dessert plate. Cut cupcakes in half; place 2 halves on top of chocolate on each dessert plate. Top each with about 2 heaping tablespoonfuls pudding. Garnish with pineapple halves and orange peel. Serve immediately.   *Makes 12 servings*

Nutrients per Serving

Calories	158	Saturated Fat	1 g	Cholesterol	29 mg
Calories from Fat	22 %	Protein	3 g	Sodium	175 mg
Total Fat	4 g	Carbohydrate	28 g	Dietary Fiber	<1 g

DIETARY EXCHANGES: 2 Starch, ½ Fat

Boston Baby

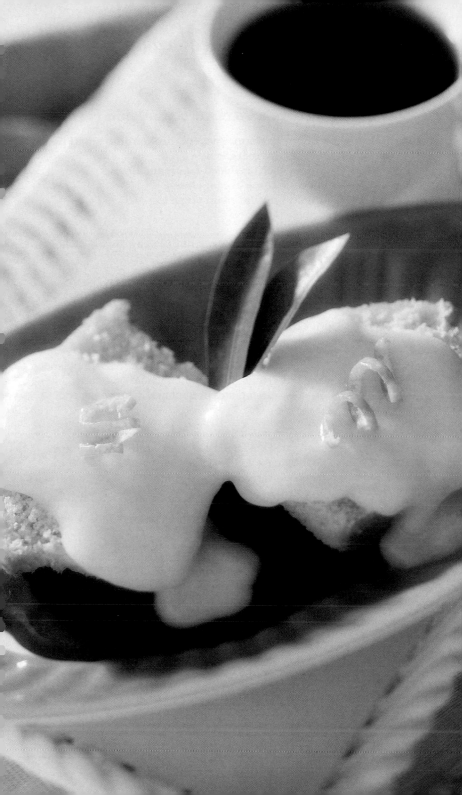

Key Lime Cheesecake with Strawberries and Fresh Mint

12 whole low-fat honey graham crackers, broken into small pieces
2 tablespoons reduced-fat margarine
2 packages (8 ounces each) reduced-fat cream cheese
1 package (8 ounces) fat-free cream cheese
1 container (8 ounces) nonfat plain yogurt
⅔ cup powdered sugar
¼ cup lime juice
8 packets sugar substitute *or* equivalent of ⅓ cup sugar, divided
2 teaspoons lime peel
1½ teaspoons vanilla
3 cups fresh strawberries, quartered
2 tablespoons finely chopped mint leaves

1. Preheat oven 350°F. Coat 9-inch springform baking pan with nonstick cooking spray; set aside.

2. Place graham cracker pieces and margarine in food processor or blender; pulse until coarse in texture. Gently press crumb mixture on bottom and up ½ inch side of pan. Bake 8 to 10 minutes or until lightly browned; cool completely on wire rack.

3. Beat cream cheese, yogurt, powdered sugar, lime juice, 6 packets sugar substitute, lime peel and vanilla in large bowl with electric mixer at high speed until smooth. Pour into cooled pie crust. Cover with plastic wrap; freeze 2 hours or refrigerate overnight.

4. Combine strawberries, remaining 2 packets sugar substitute and mint in medium bowl 30 minutes before serving; set aside. Just before serving, spoon strawberry mixture over cheesecake. *Makes 12 servings*

Nutrients per Serving

Calories	176	Saturated Fat	5 g	Cholesterol	20 mg
Calories from Fat	39 %	Protein	8 g	Sodium	341 mg
Total Fat	7 g	Carbohydrate	18 g	Dietary Fiber	1 g

DIETARY EXCHANGES: 1 Starch, 1 Lean Meat, 1 Fat

*Key Lime Cheesecake with Strawberries
and Fresh Mint*

Pies & Such

Frozen Sundae Pie

26 chocolate wafer cookies
4 cups fat-free ice cream, slightly softened
2 tablespoons fat-free hot fudge ice cream topping
1 cup banana slices
2 tablespoons fat-free caramel ice cream topping
1 ounce reduced-fat dry roasted peanuts, crushed

1. Place cookies on bottom and around side of 9-inch pie pan. Carefully spoon ice cream into pie pan; cover with plastic wrap. Freeze 2 hours or overnight or until firm.

2. Just before serving, place fudge topping in small microwavable bowl; microwave at HIGH 10 seconds. Drizzle pie with fudge topping; top with banana slices. Place caramel topping in small microwavable bowl; microwave at HIGH 10 seconds. Drizzle over bananas; sprinkle with peanuts.

Makes 8 servings

Note: If desired, the pie may be assembled the night before without the bananas. Top pie with bananas at time of serving.

Nutrients per Serving

Calories	252	Saturated Fat	1 g	Cholesterol	<1 mg
Calories from Fat	16 %	Protein	7 g	Sodium	210 mg
Total Fat	5 g	Carbohydrate	49 g	Dietary Fiber	1 g

DIETARY EXCHANGES: 3 Starch, 1 Fat

Frozen Sundae Pie

Provençal Apple-Walnut Crumb Pie

5 cups peeled and thinly sliced Red Delicious apples
1 tablespoon lemon juice
¾ teaspoon vanilla
½ cup packed dark brown sugar
⅓ cup plus 3 tablespoons all-purpose flour, divided
1 teaspoon ground cinnamon
¼ teaspoon ground nutmeg
1 frozen reduced-fat pie crust
¼ cup chopped walnuts
2 tablespoons granulated sugar
2 tablespoons cold margarine, cut into small pieces

1. Preheat oven 425°F. Place baking sheet in oven while preheating.

2. Combine, apples, lemon juice and vanilla in large bowl; set aside.

3. Combine brown sugar, 3 tablespoons flour, cinnamon and nutmeg in medium bowl; blend thoroughly. Add brown sugar mixture to apple mixture; toss to coat. Spoon into pie crust; set aside.

4. Heat 10-inch nonstick skillet over medium-high heat until very hot. Add nuts; cook 2 minutes, stirring constantly with wooden spoon until lightly browned and fragrant. Remove from heat; set aside.

5. Combine remaining ⅓ cup flour and granulated sugar in small bowl. Cut in margarine using pastry blender or two knives until mixture resembles course crumbs; sprinkle evenly over pie. Top with walnuts.

6. Bake 35 to 40 minutes or until bubbly and apples are tender in center.

Makes 8 servings

Nutrients per Serving

Calories	292	Saturated Fat	2 g	Cholesterol	0 mg
Calories from Fat	33 %	Protein	3 g	Sodium	135 mg
Total Fat	11 g	Carbohydrate	49 g	Dietary Fiber	3 g

DIETARY EXCHANGES: 2 Starch, 1 Fruit, 2 Fat

Provençal Apple-Walnut Crumb Pie

Rustic Cranberry-Pear Galette

¼ cup granulated sugar, divided
1 tablespoon plus 1 teaspoon cornstarch
2 teaspoons ground cinnamon or apple pie spice
4 cups peeled, thinly sliced Bartlett pears
¼ cup dried cranberries
1 teaspoon vanilla
¼ teaspoon almond extract (optional)
1 refrigerated pie crust, at room temperature
1 egg white
1 tablespoon water

1. Preheat oven to 450°F. Coat pizza pan or baking sheet with nonstick cooking spray; set aside.

2. Combine all but 1 teaspoon sugar, cornstarch and cinnamon in medium bowl; blend well. Add pears, cranberries, vanilla and almond extract; toss to coat.

3. Remove crust from pouch; unfold crust and remove plastic sheets. Place on prepared pan. Spoon pear mixture in center of crust to within 2 inches from edge. Fold edge of crust 2 inches over pear mixture; crimp slightly.

4. Combine egg white and water in small bowl; whisk until well blended. Brush outer edges of pie crust with egg white mixture; sprinkle with remaining 1 teaspoon sugar.

5. Bake 25 minutes or until pears are tender and crust is golden brown. If edges brown too quickly, cover with foil after 15 minutes of baking. Cool on wire rack 30 minutes.

Makes 8 servings

Nutrients per Serving

Calories	227	Saturated Fat	3 g	Cholesterol	5 mg
Calories from Fat	28 %	Protein	1 g	Sodium	147 mg
Total Fat	7 g	Carbohydrate	41 g	Dietary Fiber	4 g

DIETARY EXCHANGES: 2 Starch, ½ Fruit, 1 Fat

Rustic Cranberry-Pear Galette

Apple Crisp

5 cups thinly sliced Granny Smith apples
1 cup apple cider
½ cup fat-free butterscotch ice cream topping, divided
¼ cup all-purpose flour
1 teaspoon ground cinnamon
3 cups low-fat granola with raisins
3 tablespoons margarine or butter, melted
   Low-fat, no-sugar-added ice cream (optional)

1. Preheat oven to 350°F. Lightly coat 8-inch square baking pan with nonstick cooking spray; set aside.

2. Combine apples, cider, ¼ cup butterscotch topping, flour and cinnamon in large bowl. Place in prepared pan.

3. Combine remaining ¼ cup butterscotch topping, granola and margarine. Dollop over apples.

4. Bake, covered, 40 to 45 minutes. Remove cover and bake an additional 15 to 20 minutes or until mixture is bubbly and apples are tender. Serve warm with ice cream, if desired.   *Makes 9 servings*

Nutrients per Serving

Calories	254	Saturated Fat	1 g	Cholesterol	<1 mg
Calories from Fat	21 %	Protein	3 g	Sodium	177 mg
Total Fat	6 g	Carbohydrate	51 g	Dietary Fiber	4 g

DIETARY EXCHANGES: 2 Starch, 1 Fruit, 1 Fat

Eggnog Banana Pie

32 reduced-fat vanilla wafers
3 bananas, divided
¼ plus ⅛ teaspoon ground nutmeg, divided
2 cups fat-free (skim) milk
1 package (8 ounces) reduced-fat cream cheese
1 package (4 serving size) sugar-free instant vanilla pudding and
**   pie filling**
½ teaspoon brandy extract
1 cup thawed frozen fat-free nondairy whipped topping

1. Line bottom and side of 9-inch pie pan with vanilla wafers. Slice 2 bananas and arrange evenly on top of wafers. Sprinkle with ¼ teaspoon nutmeg; set aside.

2. Place milk, cream cheese, pudding mix and brandy extract in food processor or blender; process until smooth. Stir in whipped topping. Spoon mixture evenly over bananas; sprinkle with remaining ⅛ teaspoon nutmeg. Cover with plastic wrap and refrigerate until ready to serve (no longer than 4 hours). Just before serving, slice remaining banana and arrange decoratively on top of pie.

Makes 8 servings

*N*utrients per Serving

Calories	214	Saturated Fat	4 g	Cholesterol	14 mg
Calories from Fat	29 %	Protein	6 g	Sodium	297 mg
Total Fat	7 g	Carbohydrate	33 g	Dietary Fiber	1 g

DIETARY EXCHANGES: 2 Starch, 1½ Fat

*To add a splash of splendor to this fabulous pie,
garnish with edible pansies. These wonderful flowers
bring fantastic color to this dessert. Be sure to buy the
flowers from a specialty produce market or supermarket
that carries gourmet produce. Never buy the flowers from
a florist as they could be sprayed with pesticide and
should never be eaten.*

Peach Cobbler

FILLING
- **6 cups sliced ripe peaches (about 6 medium)**
- **1 tablespoon fresh lemon or orange juice**
- **1 tablespoon all-purpose flour**
- **2 tablespoons sugar**
- **1 teaspoon ground cinnamon**

TOPPING
- **1½ cups all-purpose flour**
- **¼ cup plus 2 teaspoons sugar, divided**
- **1½ teaspoons baking powder**
- **½ cup fat-free (skim) milk**
- **1 egg**
- **2 tablespoons margarine or butter, melted**
- **½ teaspoon ground cinnamon**
- **No-sugar-added ice cream (optional)**

1. Preheat oven to 350°F. Coat 9-inch pie pan with nonstick cooking spray; set aside.

2. For filling, mix all filling ingredients in medium bowl; spread into prepared pan.

3. For topping, combine 1½ cups flour, ¼ cup sugar and baking powder in medium bowl. Combine milk, egg and margarine in small bowl. Add to flour mixture; stir just until flour is blended. Drop batter by tablespoons on top peach filling. Combine 2 teaspoons sugar and ½ teaspoon cinnamon in small bowl; sprinkle on top.

4. Bake 45 to 50 minutes or until toothpick inserted in center comes out clean. Serve warm with ice cream, if desired.   *Makes 9 servings*

Nutrients per Serving

Calories	201	Saturated Fat	1 g	Cholesterol	24 mg
Calories from Fat	15 %	Protein	4 g	Sodium	126 mg
Total Fat	3 g	Carbohydrate	40 g	Dietary Fiber	3 g

DIETARY EXCHANGES: 1½ Starch, 1 Fruit, ½ Fat

Peach Cobbler

Farmhouse Lemon Meringue Pie

1 frozen reduced-fat pie crust
4 large eggs, at room temperature
3 tablespoons lemon juice
2 tablespoons reduced-fat margarine
2 teaspoons lemon peel
3 drops yellow food coloring (optional)
1 cup cold water
⅔ cup sugar, divided
¼ cup cornstarch
⅛ teaspoon salt
¼ teaspoon vanilla

1. Preheat oven 425°F. Bake pie crust according to package directions.

2. Separate eggs, discarding 2 egg yolks; set aside. Mix lemon juice, margarine, lemon peel and food coloring in small bowl; set aside.

3. Combine water, all but 2 tablespoons sugar, cornstarch and salt in medium saucepan; whisk until smooth. Heat over medium-high heat, whisking until mixture begins to boil. Reduce heat to medium. Boil 1 minute, stirring constantly; remove from heat. Stir ¼ cup sugar mixture into egg yolks; whisk until blended. Slowly whisk egg yolk mixture back into sugar mixture. Cook over medium heat 3 minutes, whisking constantly. Remove from heat; stir in lemon juice mixture until blended. Pour into baked pie crust.

4. Beat egg whites in large bowl with electric mixer at high speed until soft peaks form. Gradually beat in remaining 2 tablespoons sugar and vanilla; beat until stiff peaks form. Spread meringue over pie filling with rubber spatula, making sure it completely covers filling and touches edge of pie crust. Bake 15 minutes. Remove from oven; cool completely on wire rack. Cover with plastic wrap; refrigerate 8 hours or overnight until setting is firm.

Makes 8 servings

Nutrients per Serving

Calories	231	Saturated Fat	2 g	Cholesterol	106 mg
Calories from Fat	34 %	Protein	4 g	Sodium	197 mg
Total Fat	9 g	Carbohydrate	34 g	Dietary Fiber	<1 g

DIETARY EXCHANGES: 2½ Starch, 1½ Fat

Farmhouse Lemon Meringue Pie

Mixed Berry Tart with Ginger-Raspberry Glaze

1 refrigerated pie crust, at room temperature
¾ cup no-sugar-added seedless raspberry fruit spread
½ teaspoon grated fresh ginger *or* ¼ teaspoon ground ginger
2 cups fresh or frozen blueberries
2 cups fresh or frozen blackberries
1 peach, peeled and thinly sliced

1. Preheat oven 450°F. Coat 9-inch pie pan or tart pan with nonstick cooking spray. Carefully place pie crust on bottom of pan. Turn edges of pie crust inward to form ½-inch thick edge. Press edges firmly against sides of pan. Using fork, pierce several times over entire bottom of pan to prevent crust from puffing up while baking. Bake 12 minutes or until golden brown. Cool completely on wire rack.

2. Heat fruit spread in small saucepan over high heat; stir until completely melted. Immediately remove from heat; stir in ginger and set aside to cool slightly.

3. Combine blueberries, blackberries and all but 2 tablespoons fruit spread mixture; set aside.

4. Brush remaining 2 tablespoons fruit spread mixture evenly over bottom of cooled crust. Decoratively arrange peaches on top of crust and mound berries on top of peaches. Refrigerate at least 2 hours.   *Makes 8 servings*

Nutrients per Serving

Calories	191	Saturated Fat	3 g	Cholesterol	5 mg
Calories from Fat	33 %	Protein	1 g	Sodium	172 mg
Total Fat	7 g	Carbohydrate	32 g	Dietary Fiber	3 g

DIETARY EXCHANGES: 1 Starch, 1 Fruit, 1½ Fat

Mixed Berry Tart with
Ginger-Raspberry Glaze

Mocha Cappuccino Ice Cream Pie

¼ **cup cold water**
1 **tablespoon instant coffee granules**
4 **packets sugar substitute** *or* **equivalent of 8 teaspoons sugar**
½ **teaspoon vanilla**
4 **cups frozen fat-free, no-sugar-added fudge marble ice cream**
1 **vanilla wafer pie crust**

1. Combine water, coffee granules, sugar substitute and vanilla in small bowl; stir until granules dissolve. Set aside.

2. Combine ice cream and coffee mixture in large bowl; stir gently until liquid is blended into ice cream. Spoon into pie crust; smooth top with rubber spatula.

3. Cover with plastic wrap; freeze about 4 hours or until firm.

Makes 8 servings

Variation: Omit pie crust and serve in dessert cups with biscotti.

Nutrients per Serving

Calories	201	Saturated Fat	2 g	Cholesterol	9 mg
Calories from Fat	34 %	Protein	5 g	Sodium	159 mg
Total Fat	8 g	Carbohydrate	29 g	Dietary Fiber	0 g

DIETARY EXCHANGES: 2 Starch, 1½ Fat

Blueberry Granola Crumble Pie

1 package (16 ounces) frozen unsweetened blueberries
¼ cup sugar
2 tablespoons lemon juice
1½ tablespoons cornstarch
2 teaspoons vanilla
1 frozen reduced-fat pie crust
1 cup low-fat granola

1. Preheat oven 425°F. Place baking sheet in oven while preheating.

2. Toss blueberries, sugar, lemon juice, cornstarch and vanilla to coat. Spoon blueberry mixture into pie crust; place on heated baking sheet.

3. Bake 20 minutes; sprinkle granola evenly over pie. Bake an additional 20 minutes or until pie is bubbly.   *Makes 8 servings*

Cook's Tip: If pie is allowed to stand 4 hours or overnight the flavors will blend making a sweeter tasting dessert. This is true with most fruit pies, especially blueberry, cherry and peach pies.

Nutrients per Serving

Calories	216	Saturated Fat	1 g	Cholesterol	0 mg
Calories from Fat	24 %	Protein	3 g	Sodium	126 mg
Total Fat	6 g	Carbohydrate	39 g	Dietary Fiber	3 g

DIETARY EXCHANGES: 2 Starch, ½ Fruit, 1 Fat

Company's Coming

Spun Sugar Berries with Yogurt Crème

2 cups fresh raspberries*
**1 container (8 ounces) lemon-flavored nonfat yogurt with
   aspartame sweetener**
1 cup thawed frozen fat-free nondairy whipped topping
3 tablespoons sugar

You may substitute your favorite fresh berry for the fresh raspberries.

1. Arrange berries in 4 glass dessert dishes.

2. Combine yogurt and whipped topping in medium bowl. (If not using immediately, cover and refrigerate.) Top berries with yogurt mixture.

3. To prepare spun sugar, pour sugar into heavy medium saucepan. Cook over medium-high heat until sugar melts, shaking pan occasionally. *Do not stir.* As sugar begins to melt, reduce heat to low and cook about 10 minutes or until sugar is completely melted and has turned light golden brown.

4. Remove from heat; let stand for 1 minute. Coat metal fork with sugar mixture. Drizzle sugar over berries with circular or back and forth motion. Ropes of spun sugar will harden quickly. Garnish as desired. Serve immediately.   *Makes 4 servings*

Nutrients per Serving

Calories	119	Saturated Fat	<1 g	Cholesterol	0 mg
Calories from Fat	2 %	Protein	3 g	Sodium	45 mg
Total Fat	<1 g	Carbohydrate	26 g	Dietary Fiber	4 g

DIETARY EXCHANGES: 2 Fruit

Spun Sugar Berries with Yogurt Crème

Caffè en Forchetta

2 cups reduced-fat (2%) milk
1 cup cholesterol-free egg substitute
½ cup sugar
2 tablespoons no-sugar-added mocha-flavored instant coffee
Grated chocolate or 6 chocolate-covered coffee beans (optional)

1. Preheat oven to 325°F.

2. Combine all ingredients in medium bowl except grated chocolate. Whisk until instant coffee has dissolved and mixture is foamy. Pour into six individual custard cups. Place cups in 13×9-inch baking pan. Fill with hot water halfway up side of cups.

3. Bake 55 to 60 minutes or until knife inserted halfway between center and edge comes out clean. Serve warm or at room temperature. Garnish with grated chocolate or chocolate-covered coffee bean , if desired.

Makes 6 servings

Nutrients per Serving

Calories	111	Saturated Fat	1 g	Cholesterol	6 mg
Calories from Fat	16 %	Protein	7 g	Sodium	136 mg
Total Fat	2 g	Carbohydrate	17 g	Dietary Fiber	0 g

DIETARY EXCHANGES: 1 Starch, 1 Lean Meat

Caffè en Forchetta

Cherry-Almond Phyllo Rolls

1 can (16 ounces) sour pitted cherries, undrained
⅓ cup no-sugar-added seedless raspberry fruit spread
⅓ cup granulated sugar, divided
2 tablespoons cornstarch
½ teaspoon almond extract
16 sheets phyllo dough
Butter-flavored nonstick cooking spray
½ cup sliced almonds

1. Preheat oven 400°F. Coat nonstick baking sheet with nonstick cooking spray; set aside.

2. Combine cherries with juice, raspberry fruit spread, all but 1 tablespoon sugar and cornstarch in small saucepan. Stir until cornstarch is completely dissolved. Bring to a boil over medium-high heat, stirring occasionally. Continue boiling and gently stirring one minute. Remove from heat and stir in almond extract; set aside.

3. Place 2 sheets phyllo dough on work surface. Keep remaining sheets covered with plastic wrap and damp kitchen towel. Spray top sheet of phyllo dough with nonstick cooking spray; fold in half crosswise and spray again. Spoon ⅓ cup cherry mixture to within 3 inches of bottom long edge. Fold up bottom edge. Fold in both sides. Beginning at long side, roll up jelly-roll fashion; place on prepared baking sheet. Repeat with remaining sheets of phyllo and cherry mixture. Sprinkle remaining sugar over rolls; top with almonds.

4. Bake 20 minutes; remove from oven and let stand 15 minutes before serving. *Makes 8 servings*

Nutrients per Serving

Calories	247	Saturated Fat	1 g	Cholesterol	0 mg
Calories from Fat	22 %	Protein	4 g	Sodium	201 mg
Total Fat	6 g	Carbohydrate	40 g	Dietary Fiber	2 g

DIETARY EXCHANGES: 2 Starch, 1 Fruit, 1 Fat

Baked Orange Custard with Strawberries

¾ **cup cholesterol-free egg substitute**
½ **cup sugar**
1 **can (12 ounces) nonfat evaporated milk**
¼ **cup heavy cream**
2 **tablespoons fresh squeezed orange juice**
1 **tablespoon grated orange peel**
1 **teaspoon vanilla**
2½ **cups fresh sliced strawberries**
3 **packets sugar substitute** *or* **equivalent of 2 tablespoons sugar**

1. Preheat oven to 350°F. Combine egg substitute, sugar, evaporated milk, cream, orange juice, orange peel and vanilla in medium bowl until well blended. Pour mixture into 6 (6-ounce) custard cups or ramekins. Place custard cups in 13×9-inch baking pan. Fill with hot water halfway up side of cups. Bake 30 to 35 minutes or until knife inserted halfway between center and edge comes out clean.

2. Remove from oven; let cups remain in hot water bath until they reach room temperature.

3. While custards cool, gently toss sliced strawberries with sugar substitute; set aside.

4. Serve custards at room temperature or cold. Top with strawberries.

Makes 6 servings

Nutrients per Serving

Calories	190	Saturated Fat	2 g	Cholesterol	16 mg
Calories from Fat	18 %	Protein	9 g	Sodium	128 mg
Total Fat	4 g	Carbohydrate	30 g	Dietary Fiber	2 g

DIETARY EXCHANGES: 2 Starch, ½ Lean Meat

Tropical Fruit Coconut Tart

1 cup cornflakes, crushed
1 can (3½ ounces) sweetened flaked coconut
2 egg whites
1 can (15¼ ounces) pineapple tidbits in juice
2 teaspoons cornstarch
2 packets sugar substitute *or* equivalent of 4 teaspoons sugar
1 teaspoon coconut extract (optional)
1 mango, peeled and thinly sliced
1 banana, thinly sliced

1. Preheat oven to 425°F. Coat 9-inch springform pan with nonstick cooking spray; set aside.

2. Combine cereal, coconut and egg whites in medium bowl; toss gently to blend. Place coconut mixture in prepared pan; press firmly to coat bottom and ½ inch up side of pan.

3. Bake 8 minutes or until edge begins to brown. Cool completely on wire rack.

4. Drain pineapple, reserving pineapple juice. Combine pineapple juice and cornstarch in small saucepan; stir until cornstarch is dissolved. Bring to a boil over high heat. Continue boiling 1 minute, stirring constantly. Remove from heat; cool completely. Stir in sugar substitute and coconut extract. Combine pineapple, mango slices and banana slices in medium bowl. Spoon into pan; drizzle with pineapple sauce. Cover with plastic wrap and refrigerate 2 hours. Garnish with pineapple leaves, if desired. *Makes 8 servings*

Note: The crust may be made 24 hours in advance, if desired.

Nutrients per Serving

Calories	139	Saturated Fat	4 g	Cholesterol	0 mg
Calories from Fat	25 %	Protein	2 g	Sodium	59 mg
Total Fat	4 g	Carbohydrate	25 g	Dietary Fiber	2 g

DIETARY EXCHANGES: 1 Starch, ½ Fruit, 1 Fat

Tropical Fruit Coconut Tart

Sinfully Slim Crêpes Suzette

CRÊPES
> 1 cup fat-free (skim) milk
> 3 egg whites
> ¼ cup plus 2 tablespoons all-purpose flour

FILLING
> 2½ tablespoons reduced-fat margarine
> 2 tablespoons sugar

ORANGE SAUCE
> 1 cup fresh orange juice
> 2 tablespoons sugar
> Peel of 1 orange, cut into ⅛-inch julienne strips
> 2 tablespoons orange-flavored liqueur

1. To prepare crêpes, combine milk, egg whites and flour in food processor or blender; process until smooth. Refrigerate at least 1 hour.

2. Heat 6- or 7-inch nonstick skillet over medium-high heat. Spray lightly with nonstick cooking spray. Pour 2 tablespoons crêpe batter into hot skillet; quickly rotate pan to distribute batter evenly. Cook 1 to 2 minutes or until nicely browned. Flip crêpe and cook on other side about 30 seconds. Stack crêpes on clean kitchen towel. Repeat with remaining batter, spraying skillet with nonstick cooking spray before each crêpe.

3. To prepare filling, combine margarine and 2 tablespoons sugar in small bowl; set aside.

4. To prepare sauce, combine orange juice and 2 tablespoons sugar in small saucepan. Bring to boil over high heat; reduce heat to medium-high and continue cooking until reduced by half. Add orange peel; set aside. Pour liqueur into separate small saucepan; heat over medium-high heat until warm. Light with match and immediately stop flame with lid. Combine liqueur and orange sauce; keep warm. Set aside.

5. To serve, spread each crêpe with about ½ teaspoon filling mixture. Fold crêpes in half, then in half again to form a triangle. Arrange 2 crêpes on each dessert plate; repeat with remaining crêpes. Top each serving with about 1 tablespoon orange sauce; serve warm.   *Makes 6 servings (12 to 14 crêpes)*

Nutrients per Serving

Calories	139	Saturated Fat	<1 g	Cholesterol	1 mg
Calories from Fat	16 %	Protein	4 g	Sodium	106 mg
Total Fat	3 g	Carbohydrate	23 g	Dietary Fiber	<1 g

DIETARY EXCHANGES: 1½ Starch, ½ Fat

Fruited Trifle

   1¾ cups fat-free (skim) milk
   1 package (4 serving size) instant sugar-free vanilla pudding and
      pie filling
   4 ounces Neufchâtel cheese, softened
   12 to 16 whole ladyfingers
   2 tablespoons cream sherry, divided (optional)
   2 cups fresh or frozen raspberries
   ½ cup thawed frozen fat-free nondairy whipped topping

1. Whisk together milk and pudding mix in large bowl. Beat in Neufchâtel with electric mixer at medium speed until smooth; set aside.

2. Place half the ladyfingers on bottom of 8- to 10-inch glass serving dish. Top with 1 tablespoon sherry. Spread half the pudding mixture over ladyfingers. Arrange raspberries over pudding, reserving a few for garnish. Repeat layers with remaining ingredients.

3. Top with whipped topping. Refrigerate 1 hour. Garnish with reserved raspberries just before serving.   *Makes 8 servings*

Nutrients per Serving

Calories	145	Saturated Fat	2 g	Cholesterol	68 mg
Calories from Fat	25 %	Protein	5 g	Sodium	122 mg
Total Fat	4 g	Carbohydrate	21 g	Dietary Fiber	2 g

DIETARY EXCHANGES: 1½ Starch, ½ Fat

Cider-Poached Apples with Cinnamon Yogurt

2 cups apple cider or apple juice
1 stick cinnamon *or* ½ teaspoon ground cinnamon
2 Golden Delicious apples, peeled, halved and cored
½ cup vanilla-flavored nonfat yogurt with aspartame sweetener
½ teaspoon ground cinnamon
½ cup chopped pecans, toasted

1. Bring apple cider and cinnamon stick to a boil in 2- to 3-quart sauce pan over high heat. Let boil, uncovered, about 25 minutes or until liquid is reduced to about 1 cup.

2. Add apples; cover and simmer about 10 minutes or until apples are just tender. Gently remove apple halves and poaching liquid from saucepan. Refrigerate until cooled.

3. Combine yogurt and ground cinnamon in small bowl; reserve 2 tablespoons. Divide remaining yogurt mixture evenly among 4 dessert dishes. Place apple halves on top of sauce. Sprinkle each apple half with toasted pecans. Drizzle with reserved yogurt mixture.

Makes 4 servings

Nutrients per Serving

Calories	159	Saturated Fat	<1 g	Cholesterol	0 mg
Calories from Fat	27 %	Protein	2 g	Sodium	21 mg
Total Fat	5 g	Carbohydrate	30 g	Dietary Fiber	2 g

DIETARY EXCHANGES: 2 Fruit, 1 Fat

To toast the pecans, spread in a single layer on a baking sheet and toast in a preheated 350°F oven for 8 to 10 minutes or until very lightly browned. Use them immediately or store them in a covered container in the refrigerator.

Cider-Poached Apple with Cinnamon Yogurt

Apricot and Toasted Almond Phyllo Cups

½ **cup low-fat (1%) cottage cheese**
4 **ounces reduced-fat cream cheese**
2 **packets sugar substitute** *or* **equivalent of 4 teaspoons sugar**
1 **tablespoon fat-free (skim) milk**
¼ **teaspoon vanilla**
4 **sheets phyllo dough**
  Butter-flavored nonstick cooking spray
3 **tablespoons blackberry preserves**
¼ **cup sliced almonds, toasted**

1. Preheat oven 350°F. Coat 8 (2½-inch) muffin cups with nonstick cooking spray; set aside.

2. Beat cottage cheese, cream cheese, sugar substitute, milk and vanilla in large bowl with electric mixer at high speed until completely smooth; refrigerate until needed.

3. Place 1 sheet phyllo dough on work surface. Keep remaining sheets covered with plastic wrap and damp kitchen towel. Lightly spray phyllo sheet with nonstick cooking spray; top with another sheet; spray with nonstick cooking spray. Repeat with remaining sheets of phyllo.

4. Cut stack of phyllo into 8 pieces using sharp knife or kitchen scissors. Gently fit each stacked square into prepared muffin cup. Bake 5 minutes or until lightly browned; cool on wire rack.

5. Place preserves in small microwavable bowl. Microwave at HIGH 20 seconds or until just melted. Spoon 2 tablespoons cream cheese mixture into each phyllo cup; drizzle 1 teaspoon melted preserves on top of cheese mixture. Top with 1½ teaspoons almonds. *Makes 8 servings*

Nutrients per Serving

Calories	109	Saturated Fat	2 g	Cholesterol	8 mg
Calories from Fat	41 %	Protein	5 g	Sodium	174 mg
Total Fat	5 g	Carbohydrate	12 g	Dietary Fiber	1 g

DIETARY EXCHANGES: 1 Starch, 1 Fat

Pumpkin Mousse Cups

1 can (15 ounces) solid pack pumpkin
½ cup low-fat sweetened condensed milk
4 packets sugar substitute *or* equivalent of 8 teaspoons sugar
1 teaspoon ground cinnamon
¼ teaspoon ground ginger
¼ teaspoon salt
1 packet unflavored gelatin
2 tablespoons water
2 cups thawed frozen low-fat nondairy whipped topping

1. Combine pumpkin, milk, sugar substitute, cinnamon, ginger and salt in medium bowl; set aside.

2. Combine gelatin and water in small microwavable bowl; let stand 2 minutes. Microwave at HIGH 40 seconds to dissolve gelatin. Stir into pumpkin mixture. Gently fold whipped topping into pumpkin mixture until well combined.

3. Spoon into 8 to 10 small dessert dishes. Refrigerate 1 hour or until slightly firm.
Makes 8 servings

*N*utrients per Serving

Calories	113	Saturated Fat	<1 g	Cholesterol	5 mg
Calories from Fat	16 %	Protein	3 g	Sodium	112 mg
Total Fat	2 g	Carbohydrate	22 g	Dietary Fiber	2 g

DIETARY EXCHANGES: 1½ Starch

These light and flavorful mousse cups are a great alternative to the traditional pumpkin pie. Serve them at holiday meals or any get-together for a wonderful treat everyone will enjoy!

Lemon Mousse Squares

1 cup graham cracker crumbs
2 tablespoons reduced-calorie margarine, melted
1 packet sugar substitute *or* equivalent of 2 teaspoons sugar
1 packet unflavored gelatin
⅓ cup cold water
2 eggs, well beaten
½ cup lemon juice
¼ cup sugar
2 teaspoon grated lemon peel
2 cups thawed frozen fat-free nondairy whipped topping
1 container (8 ounces) lemon-flavored nonfat yogurt with aspartame sweetener

1. Stir together graham cracker crumbs, melted margarine and sugar substitute in 9-inch square baking pan sprayed with nonstick cooking spray. Press into bottom of pan with fork; set aside.

2. Combine gelatin and cold water in small microwavable bowl; let stand 2 minutes. Microwave at HIGH 40 seconds to dissolve gelatin; set aside.

3. Combine eggs, lemon juice, sugar and lemon peel in top of double boiler. Cook, stirring constantly, over boiling water, about 4 minutes or until thickened. Remove from heat; stir in gelatin. Refrigerate about 25 minutes, or until mixture is thoroughly cooled and begins to set.

4. Gently whip together lemon-gelatin mixture, whipped topping and lemon yogurt. Pour into prepared crust. Refrigerate 1 hour or until firm.

Makes 9 servings

Nutrients per Serving

Calories	154	Saturated Fat	1 g	Cholesterol	47 mg
Calories from Fat	29 %	Protein	3 g	Sodium	124 mg
Total Fat	5 g	Carbohydrate	24 g	Dietary Fiber	1 g

DIETARY EXCHANGES: 1½ Starch, 1 Fat

Lemon Mousse Squares

Strawberry-Peach Cream Puffs

- **1 cup water**
- **¼ cup margarine**
- **1 cup all-purpose flour**
- **4 eggs**
- **1 quart strawberries, stemmed and quartered**
- **1½ cups diced peaches or nectarines**
- **6 packets sugar substitute *or* equivalent of ¼ cup sugar**
- **1 teaspoon vanilla**
- **½ teaspoon almond extract**
- **2 cups fat-free vanilla ice cream or 2 cups thawed frozen fat-free nondairy whipped topping**
- **1 tablespoon powdered sugar**

1. Preheat oven to 400°F. Combine water and margarine in medium saucepan. Bring to boil over high heat. Reduce heat to low; stir in flour until well blended. Remove from heat, stir in eggs one at a time until well blended.

2. Spoon 4 tablespoons batter side by side to form cloverleaf on ungreased baking sheet. Repeat with remaining batter. Bake 35 minutes or until golden brown.

3. Combine strawberries, peaches, sugar substitute, vanilla and almond extract in medium bowl. Place ¾ cup strawberry mixture in food processor or blender; process until smooth. Return to remaining strawberry mixture; set aside.

4. Once cream puffs are done, place baking sheet on wire rack; cool completely. Cut each cream puff in half crosswise. Spoon ¼ cup ice cream or whipped topping on bottom half of each cream puff. Spoon about ½ cup strawberry mixture on top of ice cream; top with top half of cream puff. Sprinkle with powdered sugar. Serve immediately.   *Makes 8 servings*

Nutrients per Serving

Calories	235	Saturated Fat	2 g	Cholesterol	106 mg
Calories from Fat	34 %	Protein	8 g	Sodium	134 mg
Total Fat	9 g	Carbohydrate	32 g	Dietary Fiber	3 g

DIETARY EXCHANGES: 1½ Starch, 1 Fruit, 1½ Fat

Strawberry-Peach Cream Puff

Pear and Raspberry Strudel

½ cup no-sugar-added raspberry fruit spread
½ teaspoon ground cinnamon
4 ripe pears, peeled, cored and thinly sliced
1½ cups raspberries
10 sheets phyllo dough (about 18×14 inches)
  Butter-flavored nonstick cooking spray
  Low-fat, no-sugar-added ice cream (optional)

1. Preheat oven to 350°F. Combine fruit spread and cinnamon in small bowl; set aside. Combine pears and raspberries in large bowl.

2. Place 1 sheet phyllo dough on work surface. Keep remaining sheets covered with plastic wrap and damp kitchen towel. Lightly coat first phyllo sheet with nonstick cooking spray. Place second sheet on top first; spray with nonstick cooking spray. Repeat process with remaining phyllo sheets.

3. Add fruit spread mixture to fruit. Spread fruit filling on phyllo to within 2 inches of edges. Starting at short sides, fold each over filling once. Beginning at long side, roll up jelly-roll fashion for roll about 14×5 inches. Place in jelly-roll pan. Lightly coat strudel with cooking spray. Cut diagonal slits about 1-inch apart and ½-inch deep along top of strudel.

4. Bake 30 minutes or until lightly browned. Cool 30 minutes. Slice diagonally into 12 pieces. Serve warm with ice cream, if desired.   *Makes 12 servings*

Nutrients per Serving

Calories	104	Saturated Fat	<1 g	Cholesterol	0 mg
Calories from Fat	10 %	Protein	1 g	Sodium	88 mg
Total Fat	1 g	Carbohydrate	23 g	Dietary Fiber	3 g

DIETARY EXCHANGES: 1½ Fruit

Lemon Yogurt Pudding with Blueberry Sauce

> 2 cups plain nonfat yogurt
> Grated peel of 1 lemon
> 2 tablespoons fresh lemon juice, divided
> 1 teaspoon vanilla
> 8 packets sugar substitute *or* equivalent of ⅓ cup sugar, divided
> 1½ cups fresh blueberries, divided
> 1 tablespoon granulated sugar
> 2 teaspoons cornstarch

1. Line strainer with cheesecloth or coffee filter and place over bowl. Spoon yogurt into lined strainer. Cover with plastic wrap and refrigerate 12 hours or overnight.

2. Discard drained liquid. Whisk together thickened yogurt, lemon peel, 1 tablespoon lemon juice, vanilla and 6 packets sugar substitute in large bowl until smooth. Cover and refrigerate 1 hour.

3. To prepare blueberry sauce, mash half the blueberries with fork. Combine mashed and whole blueberries, remaining 1 tablespoon lemon juice, 1 tablespoon granulated sugar and cornstarch in small saucepan; mix well. Cook over medium-high heat about 4 minutes or until mixture has thickened. Remove from heat and cool 2 minutes. Stir in remaining 2 packets sugar substitute.

4. Divide yogurt mixture among 4 small dessert bowls or stemmed glasses. Top with warm blueberry sauce. Serve immediately. *Makes 4 servings*

Nutrients per Serving

Calories	124	Saturated Fat	<1 g	Cholesterol	2 mg
Calories from Fat	3 %	Protein	9 g	Sodium	91 mg
Total Fat	<1 g	Carbohydrate	22 g	Dietary Fiber	2 g

DIETARY EXCHANGES: ½ Milk, 1 Fruit

Layered Fresh Fruit Jewels

1 cup cake flour
⅓ cup sugar
1 teaspoon baking powder
 Dash salt
¼ cup water
3 tablespoons canola oil
1½ teaspoons vanilla
3 egg whites, at room temperature
½ teaspoon cream of tartar
⅓ cup no-sugar-added apricot spread, strained
1 tablespoon orange-flavored liqueur or water
3 cups assorted fresh fruit, such as strawberries, kiwis, blueberries, pineapple, raspberries, apricots or plums

1. Preheat oven to 350°F. Lightly grease 13×9-inch baking pan; set aside.

2. Combine flour, sugar, baking powder and salt in large bowl. Add water, oil and vanilla; set aside.

3. Beat egg whites in large bowl with electric mixer at high speed until foamy. Add cream of tartar; continue beating at high speed until stiff peaks form.

4. Gently fold egg whites into cake batter. Pour into prepared pan; smooth surface of batter. Bake 15 minutes or until toothpick inserted in center comes out clean; cool 5 minutes. Gently turn cake out of pan; cool completely.

5. Cut cake lengthwise in half, then cut crosswise into 14 rectangles of equal size.

6. Combine spread and liqueur in small microwavable bowl. Microwave at HIGH 20 seconds or until warmed through; set aside.

7. To assemble, place 1 cake slice on each dessert plate. Brush warmed glaze on cake; top with single layer of fruit. Repeat layer ending with fruit.

Makes 7 servings

Nutrients per Serving

Calories	214	Saturated Fat	<1 g	Cholesterol	0 mg
Calories from Fat	26 %	Protein	3 g	Sodium	111 mg
Total Fat	6 g	Carbohydrate	35 g	Dietary Fiber	2 g

DIETARY EXCHANGES: 1½ Starch, 1 Fruit, 1 Fat

Index

Index

Index

METRIC CONVERSION CHART

VOLUME MEASUREMENTS (dry)

⅛ teaspoon = 0.5 mL
¼ teaspoon = 1 mL
½ teaspoon = 2 mL
¾ teaspoon = 4 mL
1 teaspoon = 5 mL
1 tablespoon = 15 mL
2 tablespoons = 30 mL
¼ cup = 60 mL
⅓ cup = 75 mL
½ cup = 125 mL
⅔ cup = 150 mL
¾ cup = 175 mL
1 cup = 250 mL
2 cups = 1 pint = 500 mL
3 cups = 750 mL
4 cups = 1 quart = 1 L

VOLUME MEASUREMENTS (fluid)

1 fluid ounce (2 tablespoons) = 30 mL
4 fluid ounces (½ cup) = 125 mL
8 fluid ounces (1 cup) = 250 mL
12 fluid ounces (1½ cups) = 375 mL
16 fluid ounces (2 cups) = 500 mL

WEIGHTS (mass)

½ ounce = 15 g
1 ounce = 30 g
3 ounces = 90 g
4 ounces = 120 g
8 ounces = 225 g
10 ounces = 285 g
12 ounces = 360 g
16 ounces = 1 pound = 450 g

DIMENSIONS

¹⁄₁₆ inch = 2 mm
⅛ inch = 3 mm
¼ inch = 6 mm
½ inch = 1.5 cm
¾ inch = 2 cm
1 inch = 2.5 cm

OVEN TEMPERATURES

250°F = 120°C
275°F = 140°C
300°F = 150°C
325°F = 160°C
350°F = 180°C
375°F = 190°C
400°F = 200°C
425°F = 220°C
450°F = 230°C

BAKING PAN SIZES

Utensil	Size in Inches/ Quarts	Metric Volume	Size in Centimeters
Baking or Cake Pan (square or rectangular)	8×8×2	2 L	20×20×5
	9×9×2	2.5 L	23×23×5
	12×8×2	3 L	30×20×5
	13×9×2	3.5 L	33×23×5
Loaf Pan	8×4×3	1.5 L	20×10×7
	9×5×3	2 L	23×13×7
Round Layer Cake Pan	8×1½	1.2 L	20×4
	9×1½	1.5 L	23×4
Pie Plate	8×1¼	750 mL	20×3
	9×1¼	1 L	23×3
Baking Dish or Casserole	1 quart	1 L	—
	1½ quart	1.5 L	—
	2 quart	2 L	—